kijc

STATE PROFILES

PENNSYLVANIA

BY REBECCA SABELKO

BARRY

BLASTOFF!
DISCOVERY

BELLWETHER MEDIA • MINNEAPOLIS, MN

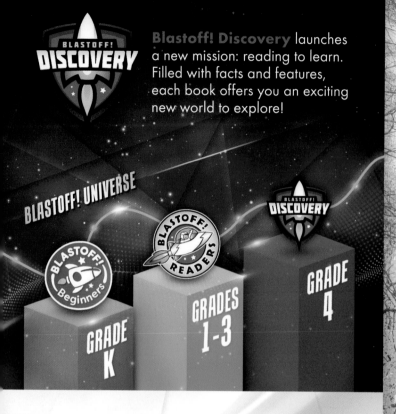

Blastoff! Discovery launches a new mission: reading to learn. Filled with facts and features, each book offers you an exciting new world to explore!

BLASTOFF! UNIVERSE

BLASTOFF! Beginners — GRADE K

BLASTOFF! READERS — GRADES 1-3

DISCOVERY — GRADE 4

This edition first published in 2022 by Bellwether Media, Inc.

No part of this publication may be reproduced in whole or in part without written permission of the publisher.
For information regarding permission, write to Bellwether Media, Inc.,
Attention: Permissions Department,
6012 Blue Circle Drive, Minnetonka, MN 55343.

Library of Congress Cataloging-in-Publication Data

Names: Sabelko, Rebecca, author.
Title: Pennsylvania / by Rebecca Sabelko.
Description: Minneapolis, MN : Bellwether Media, Inc., [2022] |
   Series: Blastoff! Discovery: State profiles | Includes bibliographical
   references and index. | Audience: Ages 7-13 | Audience: Grades 4-6 |
   Summary: "Engaging images accompany information about Pennsylvania.
   The combination of high-interest subject matter and narrative text is
   intended for students in grades 3 through 8"– Provided by publisher.
Identifiers: LCCN 2021019699 (print) | LCCN 2021019700 (ebook) |
   ISBN 9781644873434 (library binding) | ISBN 9781648341861 (ebook)
Subjects: LCSH: Pennsylvania–Juvenile literature.
Classification: LCC F149.3 .S23 2022 (print) | LCC F149.3 (ebook) |
   DDC 974.8–dc23
LC record available at https://lccn.loc.gov/2021019699
LC ebook record available at https://lccn.loc.gov/2021019700

Text copyright © 2022 by Bellwether Media, Inc. BLASTOFF! DISCOVERY
and associated logos are trademarks and/or registered trademarks of
Bellwether Media, Inc.

Editor: Kate Moening   Designer: Jeffrey Kollock

Printed in the United States of America, North Mankato, MN.

◼ TABLE OF CONTENTS

HERSHEY'S
SINCE 1894
MILK CHOCOLATE
NET WT
1.55 OZ (43g)

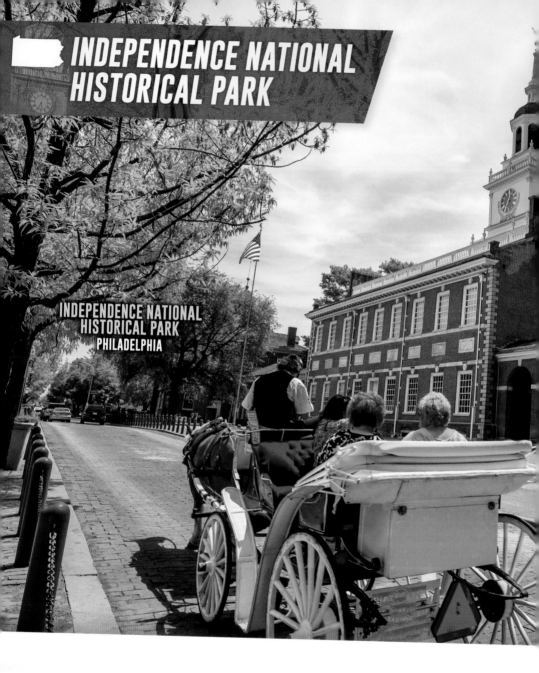

INDEPENDENCE NATIONAL HISTORICAL PARK

INDEPENDENCE NATIONAL
HISTORICAL PARK
PHILADELPHIA

It is a bright spring morning in Philadelphia. A family is ready to explore history as they head to Independence National Historical Park. They cross a brick-paved street. Independence Hall stands tall before them. They are ready for their tour!

CARNEGIE MUSEUM OF NATURAL HISTORY

GETTYSBURG NATIONAL MILITARY PARK

LAUREL CAVERNS

SEVEN TUBS NATURE AREA

The family's tour guide explains the building's important past. The **Declaration of Independence** and the United States **Constitution** were approved and signed within its walls. After the tour, the family visits the Liberty Bell. They quietly admire the bell. They think about the freedom it represents for many Americans. U.S. history comes alive in Pennsylvania!

5

Pennsylvania is in the northeastern United States. This rectangle-shaped state covers 46,054 square miles (119,279 square kilometers). Harrisburg, the capital city, lies in the southeast along the Susquehanna River.

The shores of Lake Erie line northwestern Pennsylvania. New York spans the straight northern border. The Delaware River cuts a jagged line down the state's eastern side. It separates Pennsylvania from New Jersey. Delaware and Maryland are neighbors to the south. West Virginia hugs the state's southwestern corner. Ohio lies to the west.

LAKE ERIE

OHIO

PITTSBURGH

WEST VIRGINIA

NEW YORK

PENNSYLVANIA

DELAWARE RIVER

SUSQUEHANNA RIVER

HARRISBURG

PHILADELPHIA

NEW JERSEY

MARYLAND

DELAWARE

VIRGINIA

7

IROQUOIS SETTLEMENT

People arrived in present-day Pennsylvania thousands of years ago. These early residents hunted large animals and gathered plants and berries from the land. In time, people began growing crops. Native American tribes such as the Lenape, Susquehannock, and several Iroquois groups grew.

Swedish and Dutch **immigrants** arrived in the region in the 17th century. They brought **enslaved** peoples from Africa by the mid-1600s. In the 1680s, **Quakers** moved into the area. By the late 1700s, Pennsylvania was an important **colony**. It became the second state in 1787. More immigrants arrived during the **Industrial Revolution**. Many came from Italy, Poland, and Russia.

NAMESAKE

In 1682, Englishman William Penn settled in Pennsylvania. King Charles II named the land after Penn's father. He included the Latin word *sylvania*, meaning "woodlands."

NATIVE PEOPLES OF PENNSYLVANIA

LENAPE

- Original lands in eastern Pennsylvania
- Descendants largely in the Delaware Nation in Oklahoma
- Also called Lenni-Lenape and Delaware

SUSQUEHANNOCK

- Original lands in central Pennsylvania
- No known groups remain, though descendants may be part of the Seneca-Cayuga nation in Oklahoma
- Also called Conestoga

IROQUOIS CONFEDERACY

- Original lands in northern Pennsylvania
- A group of six separate nations: Oneida, Tuscarora, Seneca, Cayuga, Onandaga, and Mohawk
- Descendants largely in Canada, New York, and Oklahoma
- Also called Six Nations and Haudenosaunee Confederacy

Pennsylvania features high mountains, deep rivers, and rolling hills. The Delaware River runs along the eastern border. Rolling **plateaus** make up southeastern Pennsylvania. They rise into the Pocono Mountains in the northeast. The Appalachian Mountains slice through the center of the state. The Allegheny Plateau covers much of the northern and western areas. The land drops toward Lake Erie.

DELAWARE RIVER

ALLEGHENY PLATEAU
APPALACHIAN MOUNTAINS

N
W + E
S

WORLDS END STATE PARK
ALLEGHENY PLATEAU

DINGMANS FALLS
POCONO MOUNTAINS

SPRING
HIGH: 60°F (16°C)
LOW: 40°F (4°C)

SUMMER
HIGH: 82°F (28°C)
LOW: 62°F (17°C)

FALL
HIGH: 63°F (17°C)
LOW: 45°F (7°C)

WINTER
HIGH: 39°F (4°C)
LOW: 24°F (-4°C)

°F = degrees Fahrenheit
°C = degrees Celsius

Pennsylvania has a **continental** climate. Summers are hot, while winters are cold. Climate change is making Pennsylvania's weather warmer and wetter. Heavy rains lead to flooding each year.

11

BLACK BEAR

Wildlife flourishes in Pennsylvania's many forests and grasslands. Black bears, cottontail rabbits, and white-tailed deer make their homes in the woodlands. They share land with noisy pileated woodpeckers and ruffed grouse. In the grasslands, mice and shrews hide from kestrels and timber rattlesnakes.

Pennsylvania is home to wetlands filled with green frogs, bass, bluegills, and wood ducks. Thousands of snow geese and tundra swans fill the southeastern waterways each spring. These birds **migrate** across Lake Erie each year. They stop to rest along Pennsylvania's shores.

EASTERN COTTONTAIL

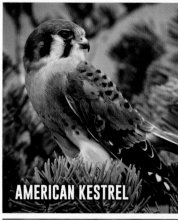
AMERICAN KESTREL

WHITE-TAILED DEER

TUNDRA SWAN

PENNSYLVANIA'S FUTURE: DISAPPEARING WILDLIFE

Pennsylvania is a leader in building urban areas. But natural spaces are destroyed as cities grow. Urban areas also introduce more pollution. Much of Pennsylvania's wildlife is disappearing as cities expand.

RUFFED GROUSE

Life Span: up to 8 years
Status: least concern

ruffed grouse range =

LEAST CONCERN	NEAR THREATENED	VULNERABLE	ENDANGERED	CRITICALLY ENDANGERED	EXTINCT IN THE WILD	EXTINCT

Pennsylvania is home to around 13 million people. About 8 out of every 10 Pennsylvanians live in **urban** areas. Most live in or near Philadelphia and Pittsburgh.

PITTSBURGH

PENNSYLVANIA DUTCH

Some groups in the state are called Pennsylvania Dutch. But they are actually descendants of Germans! They settled in the area during the 1600s and 1700s. Many still hold traditional values, such as avoiding electronics.

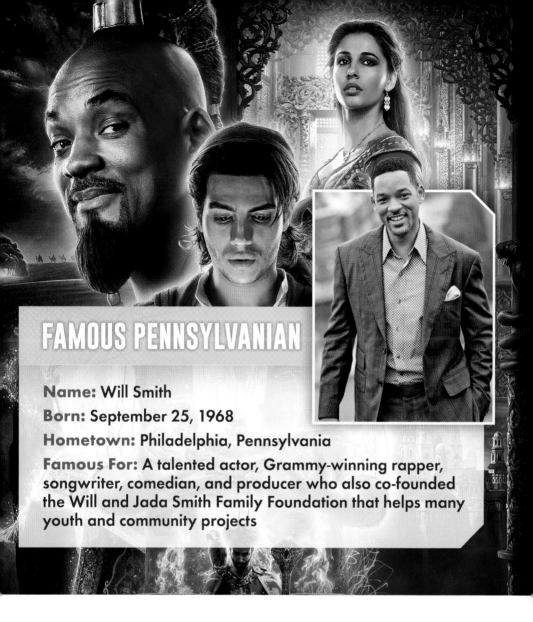

FAMOUS PENNSYLVANIAN

Name: Will Smith
Born: September 25, 1968
Hometown: Philadelphia, Pennsylvania
Famous For: A talented actor, Grammy-winning rapper, songwriter, comedian, and producer who also co-founded the Will and Jada Smith Family Foundation that helps many youth and community projects

Most Pennsylvanians are **descendants** of Europeans. The largest groups have German, Irish, Italian, English, or Polish backgrounds. Black or African Americans make up the next-largest group. Pennsylvania is also home to smaller numbers of people with Hispanic and Asian backgrounds. Many recent immigrants have arrived from India and the Dominican Republic.

In 1682, William Penn founded Philadelphia. He wanted the city to be a place of freedom for English Quakers. Philadelphia soon became the largest colonial city. It grew into a **manufacturing** center throughout the 1800s and 1900s.

Today, Philadelphia's manufacturing roots are still strong. The city also has a lively arts scene. The Philadelphia Museum of Art holds some of the world's finest collections. The Philadelphia Orchestra delights listeners around the world. Philadelphia is also known for its restaurants. Chinatown is a favorite stop for food. The Italian neighborhood, Bella Vista, draws hungry crowds as well.

PHILADELPHIA ORCHESTRA

STEEL MANUFACTURING
PITTSBURGH

In Pennsylvania's early years, the state's rich soil helped the economy grow. Steel manufacturing took over as the main source of jobs in the 1800s and into the mid-1900s. **Tourism** became more important in the 1900s.

PENNSYLVANIA'S FUTURE: RENEWABLE ENERGY

Pennsylvania is a large producer of nonrenewable energy, such as coal. But the state is shifting to more renewable sources, such as wind energy. Pennsylvania needs to develop renewable energy sources while protecting people's jobs.

Manufacturing continues to be a key part of the state's economy. Steel is still important. Companies also print books, produce chemicals, and process food. Most Pennsylvanians today have **service jobs**. Many work in advertising, banking, and **public relations**. Farming still plays a role in Pennsylvania's economy. Farmers grow mushrooms, corn, and apples.

INVENTED IN PENNSYLVANIA

SLINKY
Date Invented: 1943
Inventor: Richard T. James

BUBBLE GUM
Date Invented: 1928
Inventor: Walter Diemer

PENCIL WITH A BUILT-IN ERASER
Date Invented: 1858
Inventor: Hymen Lipman

EMOTICON
Date Invented: 1982
Inventor: Dr. Scott Fahlman

SHOOFLY PIE

Pennsylvanians enjoy many **traditional** foods. German immigrants introduced soft pretzels. These are often served with mustard. The Pennsylvania Dutch are famous for scrapple. This breakfast includes pork scraps and cornmeal that are formed into a loaf. Another Pennsylvania Dutch favorite is shoofly pie. This breakfast treat is made with molasses.

CHOCOLATE LEADER

Pennsylvania is home to The Hershey Company. It is the leading chocolate maker in the U.S.!

Italians popularized hoagies in Pennsylvania. These large sandwiches include different meats, cheeses, and veggies on a large roll. Tomato pie is an Italian pizza dish with a hint of cheese. Philadelphia cheesesteaks are known around the nation. They include thinly sliced beef and cheese. People may add onions and peppers, too.

PHILADELPHIA CHEESESTEAK

TOMATO PIE

SOFT PRETZELS

20 SMALL PRETZELS

Ask an adult to help you make this soft, chewy treat!

INGREDIENTS

1 tablespoon instant yeast

1 1/2 cups warm water

1 tablespoon honey

1 tablespoon salt, plus more for sprinkling

4 cups flour

1 egg

DIRECTIONS

1. Preheat the oven to 425 degrees Fahrenheit (218 degrees Celsius).

2. Combine the yeast, warm water, honey, and salt in a large bowl.

3. Stir in the flour and mix for a few minutes until a dough forms.

4. Pull off pieces of dough and shape the pieces into letters, hearts, animals, little bites, or any other shape you wish.

5. Mix the egg with a small amount of water in a separate bowl. Brush the egg wash over the shapes of dough, and sprinkle them with salt.

6. Bake for 15 minutes.

7. Allow the pretzels to cool, then enjoy!

Pennsylvania has more than 100 state parks and millions of acres of forests. Many people hike and bike on the state's numerous trails. Fishing and whitewater rafting are favorite water sports. In winter, Pennsylvanians often enjoy skiing and snowboarding.

Many Pennsylvanians enjoy performing arts at the state's theaters. The Pittsburgh Symphony Orchestra offers beautiful music. Locals and tourists explore the Philadelphia Zoo and Hershey Park. They can learn about history at sites such as the Flight 93 National Memorial.

PRO CITIES

Both Philadelphia and Pittsburgh are home to professional baseball, football, and hockey teams! Philadelphia also has professional basketball and soccer teams.

NOTABLE SPORTS TEAM

Pittsburgh Steelers
Sport: National Football League
Started: 1933
Place of Play: Heinz Field

Pennsylvanians kick off each new year with the colorful Mummers Parade in Philadelphia. Around ten thousand people dress in decorated costumes. String bands play instruments. Groups perform dances in the streets. On February 2 each year, the nation looks to Pennsylvania for Groundhog Day. A groundhog named Punxsutawney Phil predicts if spring will come early.

Each July, the Gettysburg **Civil War** Battle **Reenactment** honors U.S. history. The event includes mock battles with real weapons, uniforms, and more. Pennsylvanians have much to celebrate all year long!

GETTYSBURG CIVIL WAR BATTLE REENACTMENT

GERMAN CHRISTMAS

Many Pennsylvanians prepare for the holiday season with Christkindlmarkts. These traditional German markets appear in November and December. They feature food, festive performances, and much more!

MUMMERS PARADE

1776

The Declaration of Independence is signed in Philadelphia

1682

William Penn settles in Pennsylvania

MID-1700s

Native American tribes in eastern Pennsylvania are forced westward, fleeing disease and colonization

1863

The Union Army defeats the Confederate Army during the Civil War's Battle of Gettysburg near Harrisburg, Pennsylvania

1768

The colonies enact the first of a series of treaties that would remove all land in Pennsylvania from Native Americans

1952

Testing for the first polio vaccine begins at the University of Pittsburgh

2001

On September 11, 40 passengers and crew on Flight 93 prevent a terrorist attack on the U.S. Capitol as they crash the airliner in a Pennsylvanian field

1979

An accident at the Three Mile Island nuclear power plant causes part of the plant to melt and releases dangerous gases into the air

2018

The NFL's Philadelphia Eagles win Super Bowl LII, their first championship win since 1960

1879

Richard Henry Pratt opens the Carlisle Indian Industrial School where 10,000 Native American children over the course of nearly 40 years are forced to erase their culture

Nickname: The Keystone State

Motto: "Virtue, Liberty, and Independence"

Date of Statehood: December 12, 1787 (the 2nd state)

Capital City: Harrisburg ⭐

Other Major Cities: Philadelphia, Pittsburgh

Area: 46,054 square miles (119,279 square kilometers); Pennsylvania is the 33rd largest state.

Population

13,002,700

(2020)

STATE FLAG

Pennsylvania's flag has a dark blue background with the state seal in the center. Two black horses hold up the coat of arms. A ship is pictured at the top of the coat of arms. It stands for the state's industry. Below the ship is a plow and bushels of wheat that symbolize agriculture. A bald eagle sits on top of the coat of arms while the state motto, "Virtue, Liberty, and Independence," appears below.

INDUSTRY

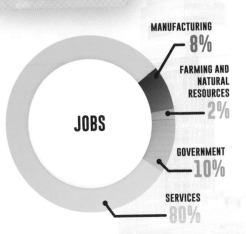

MANUFACTURING
8%

FARMING AND
NATURAL
RESOURCES
2%

JOBS

GOVERNMENT
10%

SERVICES
80%

Main Exports

coal

medications

propane

aircraft

Natural Resources
coal, oil, natural gas, timber, water

GOVERNMENT

Federal Government
17 | **2**
REPRESENTATIVES | SENATORS

19
ELECTORAL
VOTES

USA

PA

State Government
203 | **50**
REPRESENTATIVES | SENATORS

STATE SYMBOLS

STATE BIRD
RUFFED GROUSE

STATE ANIMAL
WHITE-TAILED DEER

STATE FLOWER
MOUNTAIN LAUREL

STATE TREE
EASTERN HEMLOCK

Civil War—a war between the Northern (Union) and Southern (Confederate) states that lasted from 1861 to 1865

colony—a distant territory which is under the control of another nation

constitution—the basic laws and principles of a nation

continental—referring to a climate that has hot summers and cold winters, such as those found in central North America and Asia

Declaration of Independence—a document that was signed on July 4, 1776, that stated the 13 North American colonies were free from British rule

descendants—people related to a person or group of people who lived at an earlier time

enslaved—to be considered property and forced to work for no pay

immigrants—people who move to a new country

Industrial Revolution—a period in U.S. history during the 1700s and 1800s when the economy shifted from farming to manufacturing

manufacturing—a field of work in which people use machines to make products

migrate—to travel from one place to another, often with the seasons

plateaus—areas of flat, raised land

public relations—the business of putting out information about a person or company that makes people think well of them

Quakers—members of a Christian religious group; Quakers dress in simple clothes, are against violence, and have meetings without any priests or special ceremonies.

reenactment—the acting out of a past event

service jobs—jobs that perform tasks for people or businesses

tourism—the business of people traveling to visit other places

traditional—related to customs, ideas, or beliefs handed down from one generation to the next

urban—related to cities and city life

AT THE LIBRARY

Loh-Hagan, Virginia. *Union Triumph: Battle of Gettysburg*. Ann Arbor, Mich.: Cherry Lake Publishing, 2019.

Markovics, Joy. *Horrors in Pennsylvania*. Minneapolis, Minn.: Bearport Publishing Company, 2021.

Mattern, Joanne. *It's Great to be a Fan in Pennsylvania*. Lake Elmo, Minn.: Focus Readers, 2019.

ON THE WEB

FACTSURFER

Factsurfer.com gives you a safe, fun way to find more information.

1. Go to www.factsurfer.com.

2. Enter "Pennsylvania" into the search box and click 🔍.

3. Select your book cover to see a list of related content.

INDEX